EASY ENGLISH

Romance

SHORT STORIES

JENNY GOLDMANN

BELLANOVA

MELBOURNE · SOFIA · BERLIN

Short Romance Stories

in Easy English

www.bellanovabooks.com/languages

Copyright © 2026 by Jenny Goldmann

Imprint: Bellanova Books

All rights reserved. No part of this book may be reproduced in any form by any electronic or mechanical means including photocopying, recording, or information storage and retrieval without permission in writing from the author.

ISBN: 9786192641320
Imprint: Bellanova Books

Contents

Introduction	4
Romance Vocabulary	8
The Language of Love	12
A Star-Crossed Melody	27
Lost and Found	43
The Recipe for Love	57
One for the Books	71
The Lighthouse Keeper's Love	85
Under the Moonlit Sky	103
The Love Potion	118
Sunny with a Chance of Love	132
Journey of the Intertwined Souls	147
Free Bonus Story	162

Introduction

Welcome to Easy English Romance Short Stories.

This book is written for intermediate English learners who want to improve their reading skills while enjoying beautiful romance stories.

Inside, you'll find ten short love stories written in clear, natural English. The language is simple but not childish, making it ideal for adult learners who want to feel more confident reading in English without stopping every sentence to check a dictionary.

The stories focus on everyday emotions and relationships—meeting someone new, building a connection, dealing with misunderstandings, and finding happiness in small moments. Each story is short enough to read in one sitting, so you can enjoy reading even when you don't have much time.

Learning support in every story

This book is not only for reading pleasure. After each story, you'll find:

• A short vocabulary list with useful words and expressions
• A quiz to check your understanding
• Discussion and writing questions to help you think and speak in English

These activities are designed to help you remember what you read and use new English more confidently.

INTRODUCTION

How to use this book

You can read this book in many ways, but here are some simple tips to help you learn more effectively:

Read regularly
Try to read a little every day or a few times a week. Regular reading will slowly improve your vocabulary, grammar, and reading speed.

Don't worry about every word
You don't need to understand everything. Focus on the story. If a word appears many times, write it down and look it up later.

Take notes
Write down new words, phrases, or sentence patterns you like or want to remember.

Practice speaking and writing
Use the discussion questions to speak or write about the story. You can do this alone or with a partner.

• Check your understanding
• Use the quiz at the end of each story to see how well you understood the text.

Learn with others

You are also welcome to join our Facebook group, where English learners share ideas, ask questions, and practice together.

Scan the QR code or visit:
www.facebook.com/groups/learnenglishhub

Romance Vocabulary

- **affection**: A gentle feeling of fondness or liking.
- **attraction**: A feeling of being drawn to someone, often due to their appearance or personality.
- **blush**: To become red in the face, typically as a result of embarrassment or shyness.
- **crush**: A brief, intense, and usually one-sided infatuation with someone.
- **date**: An outing or social event where two people spend time together to explore their romantic interest in each other.
- **flirt**: To behave playfully towards someone in order to express attraction or romantic interest.

- **heartbreak**: The intense sadness or pain experienced after a romantic relationship ends or when feelings of love are unrequited.
- **partner**: A person with whom one shares a romantic relationship.
- **relationship**: The connection or association between two people who are romantically or emotionally involved with each other.
- **sweetheart**: A term of endearment used to refer to someone who is loved or admired, often used to address a romantic partner.
- **admirer**: A person who has a romantic interest in or feelings of affection for someone.
- **butterflies in one's stomach**: A feeling of nervousness or excitement, often experienced when around someone you're attracted to or in love with.

ROMANCE VOCABULARY

- **candlelit dinner**: A romantic meal for two, typically enjoyed in a dimly lit setting with candles providing a soft, warm glow.
- **fall head over heels (in love)**: To become completely and deeply in love with someone.
- **first love**: The first person one experiences strong romantic feelings for; often an intense and memorable experience.
- **love at first sight**: The experience of falling in love with someone immediately upon meeting or seeing them for the first time.
- **love letter**: A written message expressing romantic feelings and affection, often sent to a person one is in love with or attracted to.

- **puppy love**: An intense but relatively shallow romantic attachment, typically experienced by young people.
- **soulmates**: Two people who are believed to be perfectly suited for each other, often sharing a deep, emotional connection and understanding.
- **steal someone's heart**: To capture someone's affection or love, usually unexpectedly.
- **tie the knot**: A colloquial expression for getting married.
- **unrequited love**: A situation in which one person has strong romantic feelings for another, but those feelings are not reciprocated.

The Language of Love

Ana, a cheerful young woman from Brazil, **nervously** walked into the classroom on the first day of her English language course. The room was filled with people from all corners of the world, each eager to learn a new language. As Ana looked around the room, she noticed a young man sitting in the corner, looking just as anxious as she felt. He was tall, with dark hair and a friendly face. Their eyes met, and he offered her a nervous smile.

"Hi," Ana said **hesitantly**, taking a seat next to him. "I'm Ana, from Brazil."

"Hello, Ana," the young man replied, his accent revealing that he was not a native

English speaker. "I'm Ivan, from Ukraine."

As the class began, Ana and Ivan discovered that they were at a similar level in their English studies. Their teacher, Ms. Thompson, put them together in a group to practice their speaking skills. Together, they stumbled through their first few conversations, laughing at their mistakes and helping each other improve.

Over the next few weeks, Ana and Ivan continued to practice together, both inside and outside the classroom. They would often visit a nearby park, where they would sit and chat for hours, trying their best to communicate in English. As they grew more comfortable with each other, they shared stories about their lives back home, their families, and their dreams.

"I want to be a doctor," Ivan said, struggling to find the right words. "I want to help people, and make them feel better."

Ana smiled, impressed by his **ambition**.

"That's a beautiful dream, Ivan. I want to be a teacher, like Ms. Thompson. I want to help people learn and grow."

As the weeks turned into months, Ana and Ivan grew closer, their conversations becoming more natural. They began to share more than just language practice; they shared their hopes, fears, and secrets. It was clear that a strong bond was forming between them, and they both felt a deep connection that went beyond words.

One sunny afternoon, as they sat in their favorite spot in the park, Ivan turned to Ana with a serious look on his face.

"Ana, I need to tell you something," he said, his voice shaking slightly.

"What is it, Ivan?" Ana asked, her heart racing with **anticipation**.

"I... I think I have feelings for you," Ivan **confessed**, his cheeks turning red. "More than just friends."

Ana's heart skipped a beat. She had felt the same way but had been too afraid to admit it. "Ivan, I feel the same way," she said, her voice barely more than a whisper.

They stared into each other's eyes for a moment, and then Ivan reached out and took Ana's hand. Their fingers **intertwined**, and it felt as if all the words they had learned in English were not enough to describe the warmth and love they felt in that moment.

As their relationship **blossomed**, Ana and Ivan continued to support each other in their language studies. They would often stay up late into the night, quizzing each other on vocabulary and grammar rules. Their shared passion for learning English only strengthened their love, and they found comfort in the knowledge that they were not alone in their journey.

One evening, as they sat on the steps of the language school, Ivan turned to Ana and said, "Ana, you make me so happy. I never thought I would find love in a language class."

Ana smiled, her eyes filling with tears. "Ivan, our love is like a beautiful dance between our hearts and our minds. We may come from different countries, and we may speak different languages, but our love is a language that **transcends** all barriers."

As the sun began to set, casting a warm golden glow over the city, Ivan pulled a small box out from his pocket. Ana's eyes widened in surprise as he opened it to reveal a delicate silver necklace with two intertwined hearts.

"This is for you, Ana," Ivan said softly. "A symbol of our love and our shared journey in learning English. These two hearts, forever connected, remind us that love knows no boundaries."

Tears filled Ana's eyes as Ivan put the necklace around her neck. She looked down at the beautiful gift, and then back up at Ivan, her heart overflowing with love and gratitude.

"Thank you, Ivan," she whispered. "I will **cherish** this always."

As the months passed, Ana and Ivan's love continued to grow, and their English skills improved dramatically. They knew that their time together in the language course was coming to an end, and they would soon have to return to their home countries. The thought of being separated weighed heavily on their hearts, but they were determined to find a way to stay together.

"I have an idea," Ana said one evening as they sat by the river, watching the stars twinkle in the night sky. "Why don't we both apply to study at a university in an English-speaking country? We can continue learning English, and we can be together."

Ivan's eyes lit up at the suggestion. "That's a brilliant idea, Ana. Let's do it."

With a positive feeling in their hearts, Ana and Ivan spent the following weeks researching universities and preparing their applications.

Their hard work paid off, and they were both accepted into a **prestigious** university in the United States. Hand in hand, they started the next chapter of their lives, ready to face any challenges that came their way.

As they **settled** into their new life together, Ana and Ivan found that their love only grew stronger. They continued to support each other, not only in their English studies but in all aspects of their lives. Through their shared journey, they discovered that the language of love was more powerful than any words could express.

Years later, as Ana stood in front of her own classroom, teaching English to a group of eager students, she often thought back to her time with Ivan in the language school. Their love story had been an unexpected and beautiful gift, born from their shared passion for learning a new language. Ana knew that she and Ivan had discovered something truly special, a love that transcended language and cultural barriers and united their hearts forever.

New Words

- **nervously** (*adverb*) - in a way that shows anxiety or apprehension; uneasily.
- **hesitantly** (*adverb*) - in a way that shows a lack of certainty or confidence; uncertainly.
- **ambition** (*noun*) - a strong desire to achieve something, typically requiring determination and hard work.
- **confess** (*verb*) - to admit or state that one has committed wrongdoing or is at fault in some way, especially to admit feelings or emotions.
- **cherish** (*verb*) - to protect and care for (someone) lovingly; to hold dear.
- **blossomed** (*verb*) - to develop or come to a promising stage, often used to describe relationships or emotions.

- **anticipation** (*noun*) - the action of anticipating something; expectation or prediction.
- **intertwined** (*adj.*) - closely connected or linked; twisted or twined together.
- **prestigious** (*adj.*) - inspiring respect and admiration; having high status.
- **settled** (*verb*) - to adopt a more steady or secure style of life, especially in a permanent job and home.
- **transcend** (*verb*) - to be or go beyond the range or limits of something; to surpass or exceed.

Test yourself

1. Where did Ana and Ivan first meet?
a) At a park
b) In an English language class
c) At a university
d) In a bookstore

2. What were Ana and Ivan's individual dreams for their future?
a) Ana wanted to be a doctor and Ivan wanted to be a teacher.
b) Ana wanted to be an artist and Ivan wanted to be a scientist.
c) Ana wanted to be a teacher and Ivan wanted to be a doctor.
d) Ana wanted to be a journalist and Ivan wanted to be a chef.

3.   How did Ivan confess his feelings for Ana?
a) He wrote her a letter.
b) He told her in the park.
c) He gave her a gift.

4.   What gift did Ivan give Ana as a symbol of their love and shared journey in learning English?
a) A pair of earrings
b) A bracelet
c) A silver necklace with two intertwined hearts

5.   What solution did Ana suggest so that they could continue learning English and stay together?
a) To become English teachers in their home countries.
b) To move to an English-speaking country together.
c) To apply to study at a university in an English-speaking country.

Discussion

1. Have you ever had a friendship or romance with someone who speaks a different language to you? What challenges did you face?

2. If you were in Ana and Ivan's situation, how would you handle the idea of being separated after the language course?

3. What do you think 'love transcends language and cultural barriers' means? Can you think of any real-life examples?

Answers:

1. b) In an English language class
2. c) Ana wanted to be a teacher, and Ivan wanted to be a doctor.
3. b) He told her in the park.
4. c) A silver necklace with two intertwined hearts
5. c) To apply to study at a university in an English-speaking country

A Star-Crossed Melody

Once upon a time, in a small **coastal** town in Australia, there lived a **talented** musician named Tom and a gifted dancer named Maria. They both came from different parts of the world. Tom was from the United States, and Maria was from Spain. Fate brought them together in this lovely town, a place where artists and dreamers could find inspiration in the gentle waves and stunning sunsets.

Tom had moved to the town to escape the chaos of the city and focus on his music. He was a pianist who could bring tears to people's eyes with his music. Meanwhile, Maria had come to the town to teach dance to children and share her passion for movement. Both of

A STAR-CROSSED MELODY

them were already very successful, but they were searching for something more fulfilling.

One day, Tom was walking down the street, feeling the warm breeze on his face, when he heard the sound of beautiful music. He followed the sound and found Maria dancing in a small **studio**. The sunlight streamed through the windows, casting a golden glow on her as she moved. Maria's eyes met Tom's as she danced, and she smiled at him. Tom was amazed by her **grace** and beauty.

"Hello, I'm Tom," he said, introducing himself after the music had stopped.

"Hi, I'm Maria," she replied with a warm smile. "Are you new in town?"

"Yes, I just moved here," Tom said. "I'm a musician."

"How wonderful!" Maria exclaimed. "I love music. Maybe we can do something together sometime."

"I'd like that," Tom agreed.

Over the next few weeks, Tom and Maria spent a lot of time together. They shared their love for music and dance, and they began to work on a duet. Tom wrote a beautiful **melody** for Maria's dance, and Maria **choreographed** an enchanting dance for Tom's music. They practiced together in the studio, their movements and notes working together seamlessly. Their duet was like a conversation between two souls, each understanding the other's thoughts and emotions.

As they worked together, their friendship grew stronger, and they began to fall in love. They laughed and shared stories, and their hearts became closer with each passing day.

Tom told Maria about his childhood, growing up in a small town in Virginia, where he learned to play the piano from his grandmother.

Maria shared her story of growing up in southern Spain, surrounded by the vibrant culture and passionate flamenco dancers who inspired her love for dance.

The connection between Tom and Maria was undeniable. They would often lose track of time as they talked, the sun setting behind them and the stars beginning to twinkle in the sky. The people in the town noticed their growing affection, and many of them would smile as they saw the couple walking hand-in-hand along the shoreline, their laughter carried away by the ocean breeze.

One evening, as they practiced their duet, Tom looked into Maria's eyes and said, "Maria, I've fallen in love with you."

Maria blushed and replied, "Tom, I love you too."

Their love blossomed, and they were **inseparable**. They spent all their time together, and the town could see the happiness they shared. Everyone looked forward to seeing their duet, which they had worked on so passionately.

As the day of the **performance** approached, Tom and Maria continued to perfect their duet. They wanted it to celebrate their love and their journey together. The anticipation in the town grew, and people spoke excitedly about the upcoming performance.

Finally, the day of the performance arrived. The whole town gathered at the small theater, eager to see Tom and Maria's duet. Friends and family filled the seats, the air buzzing with excitement. The lights dimmed, and the audience was silent.

As the music began, Maria gracefully entered

the stage. She moved like a gentle breeze, her body flowing with the music. Tom played the piano with passion, the notes filling the air with love and beauty. Together, they created a magical performance that **captivated** the entire town.

The beautiful melody Tom played on the piano complemented Maria's every step. The audience was amazed by their connection, feeling as if they were witnessing true love on stage.

The duet continued, growing in **intensity** and passion as Maria leaped and twirled, her movements a reflection of the love she felt for Tom. Tom's fingers danced across the piano keys, pouring his love for Maria into the music. The stage seemed to come alive with their passion, and the audience felt their hearts fill with emotion.

As the final notes of the duet were played, Maria landed gracefully beside Tom at the piano. They looked into each other's eyes, their love for each other shining brightly. The audience burst into **applause**, tears flowing down their faces because of the powerful performance.

Tom and Maria took a bow, their hands tightly clasped together. The love they shared had created a beautiful duet that would be remembered forever. The town congratulated them, and the couple felt a sense of **fulfillment** and joy that they had never experienced before.

In the days following the performance, Tom and Maria received countless praises from the local people. Their love story had touched everyone's hearts, and their duet was a testament to the power of love and the beauty of art.

Tom and Maria continued to live in the small coastal town, their love growing stronger each day. They continued to share their passion for music and dance, creating many more wonderful performances for the town to enjoy. The dance studio where they first met became a hub for creativity and love, inspiring countless others to pursue their dreams and believe in the power of love.

Tom and Maria also started a family, raising their children to appreciate art and the beauty of the world around them. They made sure their children understood the values of love, passion, and creativity, which they had learned throughout their lives.

And so, Tom and Maria lived out their days in the small coastal town, surrounded by their family, friends, and the beauty of the sea. Their love, which had begun as a simple connection between two artists, continued to grow and flourish until the end of their days, leaving a lasting **legacy** for future generations to cherish.

They remained an inspiration to all who knew them, proving that love knows no boundaries and can bring people from different worlds together in perfect **harmony**.

New Words

- **coastal** (*adj.*) - related to or located near the coast, where the land meets the sea.
- **talent** (*noun*) - a natural ability to do something well.
- **studio** (*noun*) - a room where an artist, photographer, or dancer works.
- **choreograph** (*verb*) - to create the sequence of steps and movements for a dance performance.
- **melody** (*noun*) - a sequence of single notes that is musically satisfying.
- **inseparable** (*adj.*) - unable to be separated or treated separately.
- **performance** (*noun*) - the act of performing a play, concert, or other forms of entertainment.
- **applause** (*noun*) - the clapping of hands by an audience to show approval or enjoyment of a performance.

- **captivate** (*verb*) - to attract and hold the attention or interest of someone.
- **fulfillment** (*noun*) - a feeling of happiness and satisfaction, especially because one has achieved something important.
- **legacy** (*noun*) - something that is a result of events in the past, often passed down through generations.
- **harmony** (*noun*) - a pleasing combination of different parts, often in music or relationships.
- **intensity** (*noun*) - the quality of being very strong, powerful, or concentrated.
- **grace** (*noun*) - smoothness and elegance of movement.

Test yourself

1.   How did Tom and Maria first meet?
a) At a concert
b) In a dance studio
c) On the beach
d) In a coffee shop

2.   What did Tom and Maria collaborate on?
a) A painting
b) A duet of music and dance
c) A book

3.   Where did Tom and Maria live?
a) In a big city
b) USA
c) Spain
d) Australia

4.   What was the reaction of the audience after Tom and Maria's performance?

a) They were bored

b) They were confused

c) They applauded and were moved to tears

d) They were indifferent

5.   What did Tom and Maria teach their children to appreciate?

a) Fame and wealth

b) Art and the beauty of the world

c) Adventure and travel

d) Science and technology

Discussion

1. Have you ever been deeply moved or inspired by a piece of art or a performance?

2. Do you think it's important to share passions with your partner? Why or why not?

3. What things in your life bring you the most joy and fulfillment?

Answers

1. b) In a dance studio
2. b) A duet of music and dance
3. d) Australia
4. c) They applauded and were moved to tears
5. b) Art and the beauty of the world

Lost and Found

Once upon a time, in the beautiful countryside of England, there was a young traveler named Sarah. She had come to this country to explore its beauty and learn about its culture. One day, while visiting a busy market, she accidentally dropped a precious **heirloom**, a necklace that had belonged to her grandmother. It was very important to her, as it was the last memory she had of her beloved grandmother.

At the same time, in a small village nearby, lived a **kind-hearted** young man named Peter. He worked in a cozy little bookstore and spent his days helping people find their favorite stories.

One evening, after work, Peter decided to take a walk by the market. As he walked, he

LOST AND FOUND

spotted a shiny object on the ground. Picking it up, he realized it was a beautiful necklace.

Peter knew that the necklace must be valuable to someone, so he decided to find its owner. He asked around the market, but nobody seemed to know who it belonged to.

Peter didn't give up. He felt that it was his destiny to return the necklace to its rightful owner.

As the days passed, Peter continued his search. He put up posters around the village and even in nearby towns, describing the necklace and asking if anyone had lost it. Meanwhile, Sarah was **heartbroken** over losing her grandmother's necklace. She had been searching for it, but with no success.

One day, Sarah saw one of Peter's posters. Her heart skipped a beat as she realized that it was her necklace he had found. Excitedly, she went to the address mentioned on the poster. As she knocked on the door, Peter opened it with a smile.

"Hello, I'm Sarah. I think you found my necklace," she said, her eyes shining with hope.

"Nice to meet you, Sarah," Peter replied warmly. "I've been trying to find the owner of this necklace for quite some time. Could you please describe it to me?"

Sarah carefully described the necklace, and Peter knew that she was the **rightful** owner. He handed the necklace back to her, and Sarah's eyes filled with tears of joy.

"I can't thank you enough for finding my necklace," she said **gratefully**. "It means the world to me."

Peter smiled and replied, "I'm just happy I could help. It seemed like fate that I found it, and I knew I had to return it to its owner."

As they talked, Sarah and Peter discovered that they had many things in common. They both loved exploring new places, reading books, and learning about different cultures.

They became friends and started spending more and more time together.

Their friendship soon turned into something more, as they realized they had a strong connection. Sarah and Peter fell deeply in love, and their relationship became a **testament** to the power of kindness and destiny. They believed that it was their destiny to find each other through the lost necklace, and they **cherished** the bond they had formed.

Together, they went on many adventures, exploring the beauty of England and beyond. They visited **historical landmarks**, tried different foods, and learned about the **traditions** of the places they went. Through every journey, their love for each other only grew stronger.

One day, while they were walking hand in hand by the river, Peter stopped and looked into Sarah's eyes. "Sarah," he said, his voice filled with emotion, "I never thought I would find someone as special as you. You've made my life complete, and I can't imagine it without you."

Tears filled Sarah's eyes as she replied, "Peter, you're the most wonderful person I've ever met. You've shown me the beauty of love, and I can't imagine my life without you either."

Peter reached into his pocket and pulled out a small box. He opened it to reveal a beautiful ring.

"Sarah, will you marry me and spend the rest of our lives together, going on adventures and making each other happy?"

Sarah's eyes widened with surprise and joy, and she nodded as tears rolled down her cheeks.

"Yes, Peter! I would love to marry you and be by your side forever."

Peter gently placed the ring on Sarah's finger, and they **embraced**, their love shining brightly like the sun. From that moment on, they knew they were meant to be together, and their love story would be one that people would talk about for many years.

Sarah and Peter's wedding was a beautiful celebration of their love, surrounded by family and friends. They exchanged their **vows** in a lovely garden, with flowers **blooming** all around them. As they looked into each other's eyes, they felt the strong bond that had brought them together.

After the wedding, they continued to explore the world, hand in hand, creating memories that would last a lifetime. They traveled to new countries, met interesting people, and shared their love of adventure with each other.

Through all the ups and downs of life, Sarah and Peter's love remained strong. They supported and encouraged each other in every challenge they faced, and their bond only grew stronger. They were known to all of their friends as the perfect example of kindness, destiny, and true love.

Years later, they would sit together, **recalling** the day when Peter found Sarah's lost necklace and how it had led them to each other. They would smile, knowing that it was fate that had brought them together and that their love was destined to stand the test of time.

The story of Sarah and Peter, the young traveler and the kind-hearted local, would always be a heartwarming reminder of how love can be found in the most **unexpected** places. And as they grew old together, their love remained as strong as ever, a shining **beacon** of hope for all who knew them.

New Words

- **heirloom** (*noun*) - An object that has been in a family for generations and is passed down from one generation to another
- **kind-hearted** (*adj.*) - Someone who is kind, compassionate, and caring towards others.
- **destiny** (noun) - The predetermined or inevitable course of events or a person's life
- **testament** (*noun*) - A clear sign or evidence of something
- **heartbroken** (*adj.*) - Overwhelmed with deep sorrow or grief
- **gratefully** (*adverb*) - With a feeling of appreciation and thanks
- **rightful** (*adj.*) - Legally or morally just or deserved

- **cherished** (*adj.*) - Held in high regard or valued greatly
- **historical landmarks** (*noun*) - Important places or structures with historical significance
- **traditions** (*noun*) - Customs or practices that have been passed down through generations
- **embraced** (*verb*) - Hugged or held closely in one's arms
- **vows** (*noun*) - Solemn promises made during a wedding ceremony
- **blooming** (*adj.*) - Having flowers or blossoming
- **recalling** (*verb*) - Remembering or bringing to mind
- **beacon** (*noun*) - A source of light or inspiration
- **unexpected** (*adj.*) - Surprising or unforeseen

Test yourself

1.   What precious item did Sarah lose at the market?
a) A bracelet
b) A ring
c) A necklace

2.   What was Tom's occupation?
a) A baker
b) A teacher
c) A bookstore employee

3.   How did Tom try to find the owner of the necklace?
a) He asked people at the market
b) He put up posters in the village and nearby towns
c) He contacted the local police
d) He posted about it on social media

4.   **What did Sarah and Tom have in common?**
a) They both enjoyed cooking
b) They both loved exploring new places, reading books, and learning about different cultures
c) They both were artists
d) They both worked in the same shop

5.   **Where did Tom propose to Sarah?**
a) At the market where they first met
b) In the bookstore where Tom worked
c) By the river during a walk
d) In a fancy restaurant

Discussion

1. Can you think of a time when a small act of kindness had a significant impact on your life or someone else's?

2. Do you believe in destiny, or do you think that Tom and Sarah's meeting and falling in love was a coincidence?

3. What do you think 'to stand the test of time' means?

Answers

1. c) A necklace
2. c) A bookstore employee
3. b) He put up posters in the village and nearby towns
4. b) They both loved exploring new places, reading books, and learning about different cultures
5. c) By the river during a walk

The Recipe for Love

In the bustling city of Detroit lived two aspiring chefs named Joanna and Sophie. They both had a passion for cooking, and they met at a cooking class. At first, they didn't get along due to their different **culinary** backgrounds—Joanna was a pastry chef and Sophie loved to cook Asian **fusion** food. But as they spent more time together, they discovered a unique chemistry and fell in love.

They worked together on a cooking competition, where they won first place, and decided to open their own restaurant. The restaurant was a huge success, and Joanna and Sophie continued to fall in love as they cooked together every day.

One day, a restaurant **critic** visited their restaurant and gave them a negative **review**. Joanna and Sophie were heartbroken, as they had worked so hard to make their restaurant a success.

Sophie was especially upset and started to blame herself for the bad review. "I knew we shouldn't have added sushi to the menu. It was my idea, and it ruined everything," Sophie said, tears in her eyes.

"Don't be silly," Joanna replied. "We're a team. It's not just your fault. We'll fix this together."

But Sophie couldn't shake off the guilt, and it started to affect their relationship. She was constantly worried about making mistakes, and it made her doubt herself in the kitchen.

Joanna noticed Sophie's distress and tried to reassure her. "You're a great chef, Sophie. Don't let one bad review bring you down. We'll work together to make our restaurant even better."

But Sophie was still struggling, and one day, she suggested they take a break from their relationship. "Maybe we should just focus on the restaurant and take a step back from our personal life," Sophie said, tears streaming down her face.

Joanna was shocked and hurt by Sophie's suggestion. "But I love you," Joanna said. "We can't just throw away our relationship because of one bad review. We're stronger together."

But Sophie was firm in her decision. "I just need some time to focus on the restaurant. We can still work together, but let's take a break from our personal life for a while."

Joanna **reluctantly** agreed, but it was hard for her to see Sophie every day and not be able to express her love. They continued to work together, but there was a distance between them that neither of them knew how to deal with.

One day, they were cooking together in the kitchen when Sophie accidentally burned a dish. She was embarrassed and frustrated with herself, and Joanna could see the tears welling up in her eyes.

"Sophie, it's okay," Joanna said, taking her hand. "We all make mistakes. We'll fix it together."

But instead of being comforted, Sophie pulled away. "I can't do this anymore," she said, her voice shaking. "I can't handle the pressure. I need to leave."

And with that, Sophie walked out of the kitchen and out of Joanna's life.

Joanna was devastated. She had lost the love of her life and her business partner. She didn't know how to move on, but she knew that she couldn't give up on her dream of running a successful restaurant.

Months went by, and Joanna continued to work hard at the restaurant, even though it wasn't the same without Sophie. She missed her every day and often wondered what could have been if they had worked through their issues.

One day, a new restaurant opened up across the street. It was run by a famous chef who had won numerous awards and had a huge following on social media. Joanna knew that she had to **step up her game** if she wanted to compete.

So she worked day and night, trying out new recipes and adding new dishes to the menu. And slowly but surely, the restaurant started to pick up business again.

One day, as Joanna was working in the

kitchen, she heard a familiar voice. It was Sophie.

"I'm sorry, Joanna," Sophie said, tears in her eyes. "I made a mistake. I shouldn't have left you. I realized that I love you and that I can't live without you."

Joanna was stunned. She didn't know what to say. All of the pain and hurt that she had been feeling for months suddenly came rushing back, and she didn't know if she could forgive Sophie for leaving her.

But as she looked into Sophie's eyes, she saw the love and **sincerity** in them. She knew that she still loved Sophie too, and that she didn't want to lose her again.

After a long conversation, Joanna and Sophie decided to give their relationship another chance. They worked together to create new dishes for the restaurant, and they were more in love than ever before.

And when the famous chef from across the street came to their restaurant to try their food, he was blown away. He declared that Joanna and Sophie's restaurant was the best in the city and that he had never tasted anything like it before.

Joanna and Sophie were overjoyed. They had worked hard to create a unique culinary experience, and they had succeeded. And most importantly, they had found their way back to each other.

As they celebrated their success, Joanna looked at Sophie and said, "You know, I think we found the recipe for love."

Sophie smiled and replied, "I think you're right. And I know that I never want to lose it again."

And with that, they shared a kiss and continued to work together, knowing that they were stronger together than they ever were apart.

New words

- **culinary** (*adj.*) - related to cooking or the kitchen
- **aspiring** (*adj.*) - having a strong desire or ambition to achieve something
- **fusion** (*noun*) - the blending of two or more different culinary traditions or styles to create a new dish
- **critic** (*noun*) - someone who evaluates and writes about food, art, or other cultural products

THE RECIPE FOR LOVE

- **sincerity** (*noun*) - honesty and genuine feelings or intentions
- **culinary background** (*noun*) - the history, experience, or training that someone has in the field of cooking
- **cuisine** (*noun*) - a particular style or type of food, often associated with a specific region or culture
- **review** (*noun*) - a critical evaluation or assessment, often of a product or service
- **strain** (*noun*) - stress or pressure on a relationship or situation, often caused by external factors or conflicts
- **to step up one's game** (*verb*) - to improve one's skills, performance, or efforts in order to meet higher expectations or compete at a higher level.
- **reluctantly** (*adverb*) - with hesitation, unwillingly, or showing doubt or hesitation in doing something.

Test yourself

1. How did Joanna and Sophie first meet?
a) At a restaurant
b) At a cooking competition
c) In a cooking class

2. What caused a strain in Joanna and Sophie's relationship?
a) A bad restaurant review
b) A disagreement over a dish
c) A personal issue outside of the restaurant

3. What did Sophie suggest to Joanna during their difficult time?
a) That they break up and focus on the restaurant
b) That they take a vacation
c) That they hire a new chef to help them

4. What caused Sophie to return to Joanna?
a) She realized that she still loved her and couldn't live without her
b) The restaurant was failing without her
c) She needed help with her own restaurant

5. What was the outcome of Joanna and Sophie's journey?
a) They opened a successful restaurant and fell in love
b) They gave up on their restaurant dreams
c) They went their separate ways and found new partners

Discussion

1. Do you think Sophie's suggestion to take a break was the right decision? Should she have reacted so strongly to the negative review?
2. What are some challenges that couples face when they work together in a business? How can they work through these challenges and maintain healthy relationships both inside and outside of work?
3. Have you ever gone back to a relationship that had previously ended? How did it work out?

Answers

1. c) In a cooking class
2. a) A bad restaurant review
3. a) That they break up and focus on the restaurant
4. a) She realized that she still loved her and couldn't live without her
5. a) They opened a successful restaurant and fell in love

One for the Books

John had always been a **solitary** person. Growing up, he preferred to spend his time lost in books, **immersing** himself in the worlds of fantasy and adventure. As he got older, he turned his love of books into a career, opening up his own bookstore in the heart of the city. Despite the long hours and occasional loneliness, he found it to be a fulfilling life.

One day, while sorting through the shelves, John came across a book that he didn't recognize. It was a worn hardback, with a faded cover and yellowed pages. Inside, he found a note from a woman named Diane.

"To whoever finds this book, I hope it brings

you as much joy and wonder as it did me. -Diane"

John was struck by the message. It was such a simple gesture, yet it made him feel seen and appreciated. He wondered who Diane was, and why she would leave a note like this. He decided to write a note back, thanking her for the message and asking her to contact him if she wanted to discuss the book further. He left the note inside the same book, but didn't expect to hear anything back.

However, a few days later, John received a reply. Diane had found his note, and was intrigued by the idea of discussing books with someone new. They started a conversation, each letter leading to more questions and insights.

John found himself looking forward to her

responses, and often spent hours writing the perfect response. They discussed books, of course, but also their lives and experiences.

John learned that Diane was an artist, who loved to paint and travel. He couldn't help but admire her bravery and sense of adventure.

Diane was equally intrigued by John's intelligence and thoughtfulness. She loved the way he would carefully read each book they discussed, always finding something new to appreciate. She found herself eagerly awaiting each letter, feeling a sense of excitement each time the mailman came by.

As their letters continued, John found himself feeling closer and closer to Diane. He found himself opening up in ways he never had before, telling her about his childhood and his dreams for the future. Diane, too, shared her innermost thoughts and feelings.

One day, John decided to ask Diane to meet in person. They arranged to meet at a nearby park. As he waited for her, John felt nervous and excited. He wondered if she would be as beautiful in person as she was in his mind.

When he saw her for the first time, he was struck by her beauty. Diane was tall and graceful, with long, curly hair and bright blue eyes. She wore a simple blue dress that complemented her eyes.

"John?" Diane said, extending her hand.

"Hi, Diane. It's nice to finally meet you," John said, shaking her hand.

They sat down on a bench, and John ordered them both coffee. They talked about books, of course, but also their lives outside of reading. John learned that Diane was much more outgoing than he had imagined. She had traveled all over the world, and had even lived in several countries.

Diane was surprised by how charming and funny John was in person. She had expected him to be more **reserved**, based on his letters, but he was actually quite **engaging**. She found herself laughing at his jokes and enjoying his company.

As they walked around the park, they came across a street musician playing a guitar. The musician was playing a beautiful song, and Diane couldn't resist dancing along. John watched in amazement as Diane swayed to the music, her eyes closed, lost in the moment.

From that moment on, they were **inseparable**. They spent all their free time together, exploring the city, visiting art galleries and museums, and talking about everything

As they spent more time together, John and Diane found that they shared many of the same passions and interests. They both loved art, music, and travel, and they were both passionate about climate change and the environment.

One day, Diane asked John to come to an art exhibit she was hosting at a local gallery. John had never been to an art exhibit before, but he was excited to see what Diane had been working on.

When they arrived at the gallery, John was blown away by the beauty and creativity of Diane's work. She had painted a series of portraits that captured the interesting characters of the people she had met during her travels. The colors were vibrant, and the **brushstrokes** were **bold** and expressive.

Diane was nervous about showing her work to John, but she was thrilled when he praised her talent and creativity.

"You're an amazing artist, Diane. You have such a gift for capturing the beauty and complexity of the world around us," he said, looking at her with admiration.

From that day on, John became Diane's biggest supporter. He encouraged her to keep working on her art, even when she faced rejection or criticism. He helped her set up her own studio, and he even offered to help her with her business plan.

As their relationship grew stronger, John and Diane decided to take a trip together. They traveled to Europe, visiting the museums and galleries of Paris, Amsterdam, and Berlin. They stayed in small bed and breakfasts, ate delicious food, and made memories that would last a lifetime.

On the last night of their trip, as they watched the sunset over the city of Berlin, John got down on one knee and proposed to Diane.

"Diane, you've brought so much joy and beauty into my life. I can't imagine spending another day without you by my side. Will you marry me?"

Diane was overwhelmed with emotion. She had never felt so loved and **cherished** in her life.

"Yes, John! Yes, I will marry you!" she said, tears streaming down her face.

They returned to **the States** and began planning their wedding. They decided to have a small ceremony, with only their closest friends and family in attendance. Diane's paintings were displayed throughout the venue, adding a personal and unique touch to the celebration.

As they exchanged their vows, John and Diane knew that they had found something special.

They had found a love that was based on mutual respect, admiration, and shared passions. They knew that there would be challenges ahead, but they were ready to face them together, with love and determination.

Years later, as they sat together on their porch, sipping tea and watching the sunset, John turned to Diane and said, "You know, I still can't believe that we met through a book. It's like fate brought us together."

Diane smiled and took his hand. "Our love story really was **one for the books**.".

New words

- **solitary** (*adj.*) - living or being alone
- **immersing** (*adj.*) - becoming fully involved or absorbed in something
- **inseparable** (*adj.*) - unable to be separated or divided
- **brushstrokes** (*noun*) - marks made with a brush in painting
- **bold** (*adj.*) - strong and confident in character or behavior
- **expressive** (*adj.*) - conveying thoughts or feelings effectively
- **cherished** (*adj.*) - valued and deeply loved
- **determination** (*noun*) - the act of making a firm decision and sticking to it
- **the States** (*noun, proper*) - the United States of America

- **one for the books** (*idiomatic expression*) - something extraordinary or exceptional, something that is worth remembering. It's often used to describe an event, experience, or achievement that is particularly memorable or remarkable.
- **reserved** (adj.): describes someone who tends to be introverted and prefers to keep to themselves, rather than being outgoing

Test yourself

1. What was John's profession before he opened his own bookstore?
a) Teacher
b) Lawyer
c) Engineer
d) None of the above

2. What was the name of the woman who left a note in the book that John found in his bookstore?
a) Diane
b) Emily
c) Sophia

3. What was Diane's profession?
a) Artist
b) Writer
c) Musician

4. What did John and Diane do on their trip to Europe?
a) Went on a cruise
b) Visited museums and galleries
c) Went hiking in the mountains

5. Where did John propose to Diane?
a) Berlin
b) Paris
c) New York

Discussion

1. Have you ever found an unexpected connection with someone? What was it like?
2. What role do you think books and reading can play in bringing people together?
3. Do you enjoy visiting bookstores and libraries, or do you prefer shopping for books online? Why?

Answers

1. d) None of the above
2. a) Diane
3. a) Artist
4. b) Visited museums and galleries
5. a) Berlin

The Lighthouse Keeper's Love

Mick was a lighthouse keeper. He lived alone in a **lighthouse** by the sea. He had always enjoyed the peace and quiet of his job, but sometimes he felt lonely. One stormy night, as he was walking on the beach, he found a woman lying on the sand. She was unconscious and he quickly carried her to his lighthouse.

Mick took care of the woman, whose name was Tracy, until she woke up. Tracy was a mystery to Mick. She didn't remember anything about how she ended up on the beach or who she was. Mick offered her shelter and food, and Tracy accepted.

THE LIGHTHOUSE KEEPER'S LOVE

As the days went by, Mick and Tracy spent a lot of time together. They would talk about everything, from their favorite books to their childhood memories. Mick was happy to have someone to talk to, and Tracy was **grateful** for Mick's kindness.

One day, Mick took Tracy to the top of the lighthouse. From there, they could see the entire coastline, and Mick told Tracy the history of the lighthouse. He explained that the lighthouse had been built many years ago to guide sailors safely to shore. Tracy was fascinated by the story, and she asked Mick to teach her how to operate the lighthouse.

Mick agreed and showed Tracy how to turn on the light and how to maintain the lighthouse. Tracy loved learning about the lighthouse and spent many hours with Mick, taking care of it.

As they spent more time together, Mick and Tracy started to fall in love. They would share meals, watch the sunset together, and read books in the cozy living room of the lighthouse. They were happy and content in each other's company.

One evening, as they were enjoying a glass

of wine by the fireplace, Tracy turned to Mick and asked, "Do you ever feel lonely, Mick?"

Mick looked at her, surprised by her question. "Of course, I do. Why do you ask?"

"I just feel like we are the only two people in the world sometimes," Tracy said softly.

Mick took her hand and squeezed it. "That's because we are. But you know what they say, 'Two is company, and three's a crowd'."

Tracy smiled at him. "I like our company, Mick."

Mick leaned in and kissed her. It was a gentle kiss, filled with tenderness and longing. They pulled back and looked at each other, their eyes shining with love.

As they sat in silence, enjoying the warmth

of the fire, Mick felt like he had found his soulmate. He had never felt so connected to another person before. Tracy was like a breath of fresh air in his lonely life, and he never wanted to let her go.

Days turned into weeks, and weeks turned into months. Mick and Tracy were happy together, and the lighthouse became their home. They would spend their days taking care of the lighthouse, walking on the beach, and exploring the nearby towns.

But their happiness was not to last forever. One day, a man came to the lighthouse looking for Tracy. He claimed to be her **fiancé**, and he demanded that she come back home with him. Tracy was confused and didn't know what to do. Mick felt hurt and jealous, but he didn't want to stand in the way of Tracy's happiness.

As Tracy packed her bags, Mick tried to be brave. "I'll miss you," he said, trying to keep his voice steady.

Tracy looked at him, tears streaming down her face. "I'll miss you too, Mick. You have been my rock in this confusing time."

Mick hugged her tightly, not wanting to let go. "Just remember, the lighthouse will always be here for you. You can come back any time."

Tracy nodded, and as she pulled away, Mick looked into her eyes and said, "I love you, Tracy. Always remember that."

Tracy's hesitated for a moment before saying, "I love you too, Mick." She then turned and walked out of the lighthouse, leaving Mick alone once again.

For the next few days, Mick was **inconsolable**. He couldn't eat, he couldn't sleep, and he spent all his time in the lighthouse, looking out to sea and waiting for Tracy to come back.

But as the days turned into weeks, Mick slowly began to accept that Tracy was not coming back. He tried to distract himself by focusing on his work, but every time he looked at the lighthouse, he was reminded of Tracy.

One night, as Mick was lying in bed, he heard a knock on the door. He got up and walked to the door, wondering who it could be at this late hour.

When he opened the door, he was surprised to see Tracy standing there, looking tired but relieved. "Mick, I need your help," she said.

Mick didn't know what to think. He was overjoyed to see Tracy again, but he didn't want to get his hopes up.

"What do you need, Tracy?" he asked cautiously.

"I need a place to stay," Tracy said. "My fiancé and I had a huge fight, and I left him. I don't have anywhere else to go."

Mick felt a surge of protectiveness for Tracy. "Of course, you can stay here," he said without hesitation. "This is your home, Tracy."

Tracy smiled gratefully at Mick, and he could see the relief in her eyes. "Thank you, Mick. I don't know what I would do without you."

Mick showed Tracy to the guest room, and she settled in for the night. As he lay in his own bed, Mick couldn't help but feel like this was his second chance with Tracy. He didn't know what the future held, but he was determined to make the most of it.

Over the next few weeks, Mick and Tracy fell back into their old routine. They would take care of the lighthouse together, go for walks on the beach, and cook meals together in the evenings. Mick didn't want to push Tracy too hard, but he couldn't help but feel hopeful that they could start a new life together.

One day, as they were walking on the beach, Mick worked up the courage to ask Tracy a question. "Tracy, do you ever think about us?"

Tracy looked at him, surprised by the question. "What do you mean?"

"I mean, do you ever think about what could have been between us?" Mick said, his heart pounding in his chest.

Tracy hesitated for a moment before saying, "Yes, I do. But I don't want to hurt you, Mick. I don't know if I'm ready for a relationship right now."

Mick nodded, feeling disappointed but not surprised. "I understand, Tracy. I just wanted you to know how I feel."

Tracy smiled at him, a sad smile that didn't reach her eyes. "I appreciate your honesty, Mick. You're a wonderful man."

As the days went by, Mick tried to put his feelings for Tracy aside. He didn't want to push her away by being too eager, but he couldn't help but feel like they were meant to be together.

One evening, as they were sitting in the living

room, Tracy turned to Mick and said, "You know, Mick, I was thinking about what you said the other day. About us."

Mick's heart skipped a beat. "What about it?"

"Well, I've been thinking a lot about us too," Tracy said, taking a deep breath. "And I've come to the conclusion that I don't want to spend my life wondering 'what if'. I want to give us a chance."

Mick felt like his heart was going to burst with joy. "Are you serious, Tracy?"

Tracy nodded, a smile spreading across her face. "I am. I don't know where this will lead, but I'm willing to find out."

Mick couldn't help but feel like this was a dream come true. He had waited so long for Tracy, and now she was finally his. He leaned in and kissed her, a passionate kiss that showed her all the love he felt for her.

Over the next few weeks, Mick and Tracy started a new chapter in their lives. They were officially a couple, and they spent all their time together. They would cook meals together, dance in the living room, and watch the stars from the top of the lighthouse.

One day, as they were sitting on the beach, Tracy turned to Mick and said, "You know, Mick, I don't think I've ever been as happy as I am now. You make me feel alive."

Mick smiled at her, feeling grateful for the love they shared. "I feel the same way, Tracy. You are my light in the darkness."

Years went by, and Mick and Tracy were inseparable. They dealt with all of life's challenges together, their love being their anchor. They welcomed a beautiful daughter into the world, whom they named Lila, after the wildflowers that grew along the shoreline. Lila grew up surrounded by love, and she inherited her parents' passion for the lighthouse and the sea.

Together, Mick and Tracy continued to take care of the lighthouse and their love for each other grew stronger every day. The once lonely lighthouse became a **beacon** not only for lost ships but also for their love, shining brightly and guiding them through life's storms.

New words

- **lighthouse** (*noun*) - a tower or building equipped with a powerful light used as a navigational aid for ships at sea.
- **inconsolable** (*adj.*) - unable to be comforted or consoled.
- **fiancé** (*noun*) - a person engaged to be married.
- **beacon** (*noun*) - a fire or light set up as a warning or signal.
- **grateful** (*adj.*) - feeling or showing gratitude or thanks.

Test yourself

1. What is the name of the lighthouse keeper in the story?
a) Jack
b) Tom
c) Harry
d) Mick

2. What is the name of the woman who Mick finds on the beach?
a) Emily
b) Tracy
c) Lily
d) Grace

3. What does Mick teach Tracy to do?
a) Cook meals
b) Dance
c) Operate the lighthouse
d) Sing

4. Who comes looking for Tracy and demands that she go back home?
a) Her father
b) Her brother
c) Her fiancé
d) Her ex-husband

5. Which of the following events happens first in the story of Mick and Tracy?
a) Tracy's fiancé comes looking for her at the lighthouse.
b) Mick finds Tracy lying unconscious on the beach.
c) Mick teaches Tracy how to operate the lighthouse.
d) Tracy decides to give her relationship with Mick a chance.

Discussion

1. In the story, Mick and Tracy find love in an unexpected place. Have you ever found love in an unlikely situation? Share your thoughts and experiences.

2. When Tracy's fiancé arrives, Mick chooses not to stand in the way of her happiness, even though it hurts him. Do you agree with his decision? What would you have done in his place, and why?

3. Would you like to live a quiet life in a lighthouse? Why or why not?

Answers

1. b) Mick
2. a) Tracy
3. c) Operate the lighthouse
4. c) Her fiancé
5. b) Mick finds Tracy lying unconscious on the beach.

Under the Moonlit Sky

Lena had always been fascinated by the stars. As a little girl, she would spend hours staring up at the sky, imagining what it would be like to explore the universe. Now, as a young woman, she was living that dream. She worked at the **observatory**, spending her nights studying the **cosmos**.

One night, as she was gazing through her telescope, she saw another **astronomer**, a man named Jack, working at the telescope next to hers. She had seen him around the observatory before, but they had never spoken. He was tall and handsome, with a serious look on his face as he studied the stars.

"Hi," Lena said, trying to be friendly. "What are you looking at?"

"Hey," Jack said, turning to face her. "Just observing the **Andromeda galaxy**. It's beautiful tonight."

Lena smiled. "Yes, it is. I love how the stars

look tonight."

They continued to chat, sharing their passion for astronomy. Lena found herself drawn to Jack's intelligence and easy smile. As the night wore on, they talked about everything from their favorite **constellations** to their dreams for the future.

Before they knew it, the sun was rising and it was time to pack up their telescopes. Lena and Jack exchanged phone numbers, promising to keep in touch. As Lena drove home, she couldn't help but think about Jack and how much she enjoyed talking to him.

Over the next few weeks, they spoke on the phone and texted each other constantly. They even started working together on a project to study the movements of a nearby star cluster. Lena was thrilled to have found someone who shared her love of astronomy.

But as they worked together, Lena began to realize that her feelings for Jack were more than just friendly. She found herself thinking about him all the time and longing to spend more time with him. She couldn't help but wonder if he felt the same way.

One night, they were working late at the observatory, studying the stars. Lena couldn't contain her feelings any longer.

"Jack, I know this might sound crazy, but I think I'm falling in love with you," she said, nervously.

Jack turned to face her, a surprised expression on his face.

"Lena, I had no idea. I feel the same way," he said, taking her hand.

They shared a passionate kiss under the

moonlit sky, their love for each other growing stronger every day.

But their happiness was short-lived. Lena's boss, Dr. Rodriguez, had noticed the **chemistry** between Lena and Jack and was not happy. He thought it was unprofessional for them to be in a relationship, especially since they were working on an important project together.

Lena and Jack tried to keep their relationship a secret, but it was difficult. They couldn't resist stealing kisses and spending time together, even during their work hours. Dr. Rodriguez became increasingly frustrated with their behavior, and tensions began to rise.

One night, while they were working on their project, Dr. Rodriguez caught them kissing in the observatory. He was furious and threatened to fire them both if they didn't end their relationship.

Lena and Jack were devastated. They didn't know what to do. They couldn't imagine being apart from each other, but they also didn't want to lose their jobs.

They talked about it for hours, trying to find a solution. Finally, Jack came up with an idea.

"What if we quit our jobs here and start our own observatory?" he suggested.

Lena's eyes widened in surprise. It was a bold move, but it just might work.

They put their plan into action, finding **investors** and deciding on a location for their observatory. It was a risky move, but they knew it was worth it to be able to be together and pursue their passion for astronomy.

Their new observatory was a huge success. People from all over the world came to see the stars through their telescopes, and Lena and Jack's research was making headlines in scientific journals. They were happy and in love, doing what they loved most.

But their success didn't come without challenges. They had to work hard to keep their observatory running smoothly, and there were times when they struggled to **make ends meet**.

They also faced criticism from some in the **scientific community**, who thought they were too young and inexperienced to be running an observatory.

Despite these challenges, Lena and Jack remained committed to each other and their dream. They worked tirelessly to improve their observatory, and their love for each other only grew stronger with each passing day.

Years went by, and Lena and Jack became well-known in the scientific community. They published several **groundbreaking** papers and were invited to speak at conferences around the world. But no matter where they went or what they achieved, they never forgot the magic of that first night they spent stargazing under the moonlit sky.

As they celebrated their tenth anniversary of being together, Lena and Jack stood outside their observatory, looking up at the stars. They **reminisced** about the past and talked about their hopes for the future.

"I never would have thought that night we spent stargazing would change my life so much," Lena said, smiling at Jack.

"I know," Jack replied, taking her hand. "But I'm grateful for every moment we've had together. And I know there will be many more under the moonlit sky."

They shared a kiss, their love for each other shining brighter than the stars above them. Lena and Jack knew that no matter what challenges they may face, as long as they had each other and the beauty of the universe to explore, they could conquer anything.

New words

- **astronomer** (*noun*) - a person who studies the stars, planets, and other celestial bodies in space.
- **observatory** (*noun*) - a place equipped for making observations of astronomical, meteorological, or other natural phenomena, typically consisting of a telescope or other instrument housed in a building with a dome-shaped roof.
- **cosmos** (*noun*) - the universe seen as a well-ordered whole.
- **constellations** (*noun*) - a group of stars forming a recognizable pattern that is traditionally named after its apparent form or identified with a mythological figure.
- **andromeda galaxy** (*noun*) - a spiral galaxy approximately 2.5 million light-years from Earth.

- **(to have) chemistry** (*noun*) - an emotional or psychological connection between two people.
- **professional** (*adj.*) - relating to or connected with a profession.
- **investor** (*noun*) - a person or organization that puts money into financial schemes, property, etc. with the expectation of achieving a profit.
- **scientific community** (*noun*) - a group of people involved in scientific research, study, or practice.
- **groundbreaking** (*adj.*) - new and innovative; introducing new ideas or methods.
- **make ends meet** (*idiomatic expression*) - to manage one's finances so that income is sufficient to cover expenses, especially in difficult situations.
- **reminisce** (*verb*) - recalling or remembering past experiences, events, or memories, often with a sense of nostalgia.

Test yourself

1. What do Lena and Jack have in common?
a) They both work at a restaurant
b) They both love astronomy
c) They both love gardening
d) They both love shopping

2. What happens when Lena tells Jack that she thinks she's falling in love with him?
a) He tells her he doesn't feel the same way
b) He becomes angry and storms out of the observatory
c) He tells her he feels the same way and they share a kiss
d) He ignores her and continues working

3.   **What does Dr. Rodriguez threaten to do when he catches Lena and Jack kissing in the observatory?**
a) He threatens to give them a promotion
b) He threatens to give them a raise
c) He threatens to fire them both

4.   **What is Lena and Jack's solution to being able to continue their relationship and their work?**
a) They quit their jobs and start their own observatory
b) They stop working on the project together
c) They pretend to end their relationship and continue to secretly see each other

5.   **How does the story end?**
a) Lena and Jack break up
b) Lena and Jack get married and have children
c) Lena and Jack celebrate their 10th anniversary together, looking up at the stars

Discussion

1. Have you ever faced challenges at work because of a personal relationship? How did you handle it?

2. What is something you are passionate about and would like to pursue in the future?

3. Have you ever taken a risk in pursuit of your dreams? What happened?

Answers

1. a) They both love astronomy
2. c) He tells her he feels the same way and they share a kiss
3. c) He threatens to fire them both
4. a) They quit their jobs and start their own observatory
5. c) Lena and Jack celebrate their 10th anniversary together, looking up at the stars.

The Love Potion

Hannah was a kind and beautiful young woman who lived in a small town in Texas. She had been single for what seemed like an eternity, and she **yearned** for a true and deep love. She often found herself daydreaming about her prince charming, wondering when she would finally meet him.

One fateful day, Hannah heard about an **apothecary**, who was rumored to have the power to create love potions. Intrigued and filled with hope, she set off to visit the apothecary in search of the key to unlocking her heart's desires. Upon entering the dimly lit shop, she was greeted by an old woman with kind eyes that sparkled with wisdom.

"My dear, what brings you to my **humble abode**?" the apothecary asked.

With a **bashful** smile, Hannah replied, "I'm looking for a love potion. I want to find my one true love."

The apothecary smiled warmly as she gently

explained, "Love potions are nothing but stories, my dear. True love can only be found within the heart, not in a bottle."

Although disappointed, Hannah listened as the apothecary continued, "Instead of seeking love, focus on loving yourself. When you truly love yourself, you will attract the love of others."

Hannah didn't quite understand, but she thanked the apothecary and left the shop with a heavy heart.

Over the next few weeks, Hannah thought about the apothecary's advice. She began to practice self-care by eating healthier, exercising, and indulging in her passions like painting and playing the piano. As she embraced her newfound self-love, she started to glow from within.

One sunny afternoon, as Hannah played a beautiful song on a piano in the park, a man named Sean happened to pass by. He was incredibly handsome, and his warm smile seemed to light up the world. Intrigued by the music, Sean stopped to listen. As the last note faded, he applauded and introduced himself.

"You have a gift," he said with a smile. "I'm Sean."

Hannah blushed and introduced herself, and they began to chat. Their conversation flowed effortlessly, and Hannah felt as though she had known Sean for a lifetime. They shared many interests, and Sean was incredibly easy to talk to.

As they strolled through the park, Hannah couldn't help but realize she had found something special in Sean. Perhaps she didn't need a love potion after all.

Over the following weeks, Hannah and Sean went on countless dates filled with laughter, adventure, and an undeniable connection. They explored museums, attended concerts, and even learned how to cook together. Never before had Hannah felt such happiness.

However, their **idyllic** romance was not without its challenges. Sean was offered a job in Chicago, and Hannah was **devastated** by the news. The thought of losing him was unbearable.

"I don't want to leave you, Hannah. But I must take this opportunity. Do you think we could make a long-distance relationship work?" Sean asked hesitantly.

Hannah was unsure, having never experienced a long-distance relationship before. Confused and heartbroken, she decided to visit the apothecary again.

Upon hearing Hannah's story, the apothecary said, "Love can be a hard journey, my dear. But true love is worth every struggle. Don't let Sean disappear without a fight. Perhaps there is a way for you to make it work."

Hannah considered the apothecary's words and realized that she couldn't let go of Sean. She loved him too much to give up. The next time they met, she poured her heart out to Sean.

"I don't want to lose you, Sean. I know a long-distance relationship won't be easy, but I'm willing to try. I love you," Hannah confessed, her eyes **glistening** with sincerity.

Sean's face lit up with a smile that warmed Hannah's heart. "I love you too, Hannah.

Let's give it our best effort."

So, Hannah and Sean started their long-distance relationship, determined to keep their love alive. They spoke on the phone daily, sent heartfelt letters, and crafted thoughtful packages to remind each other of their love. They also planned visits whenever possible, cherishing every moment they spent together.

Through the **trials and tribulations** of their long-distance relationship, Hannah and Sean's love only grew stronger.

At last, after months of separation, Sean found a new job in Hannah's town, and he decided to surprise her. With a bouquet of vibrant flowers in hand, he showed up at her doorstep, his face beaming with excitement.

"I'm back, Hannah. I couldn't bear to be

away from you any longer," Sean declared, his voice filled with emotion.

Hannah's heart soared with joy, and she wrapped her arms around Sean, holding him tightly. They were finally reunited, and it felt like a dream come true.

From that moment on, Hannah and Sean's love continued to flourish. They were grateful for the apothecary's guidance, which had led them to each other and taught them invaluable lessons about love.

Hannah discovered that true love begins within, and when you love yourself, you attract the love you deserve. She also learned that love isn't always easy, but it's worth fighting for with all your heart.

New words

- **apothecary** (*noun*) - a person who prepared and sold medicines and drugs in the past.
- **humble abode** (*noun phrase*) - a modest or simple dwelling or home.
- **yearn** (*verb*) - to have an intense feeling of longing for something, typically something that one has lost or been separated from.
- **bashful** (*adj.*) - feeling or showing embarrassment or shyness when in the presence of others.
- **glistening** (*verb*) - shining or sparkling with a shimmering light, often used to describe eyes filled with emotion.
- **idyllic** (*adj.*) - extremely happy, peaceful, or picturesque.

- **devastated** (*adj.*) - feeling or showing great shock, sadness, or disappointment.
- **trials and tribulations** (*noun phrase*) - difficult experiences or events that cause suffering or stress.

Test yourself

1. What was Hannah seeking at the apothecary's shop?
a) A magical charm
b) A love potion
c) A special flower
d) A friendship spell

2. What advice did the apothecary give to Hannah?
a) To make a wish upon a star
b) To focus on loving herself
c) To use a secret incantation
d) To write a love letter

3. How did Hannah and Sean first meet?
a) At a coffee shop
b) In a bookstore
c) While Hannah was playing the piano

4. What challenge did Hannah and Sean face in their relationship?
a) They were from rival families
b) Sean had to move to a distant city for work
c) They had conflicting work schedules
d) They disagreed about their future goals

5. What important lesson did Hannah learn from the apothecary's advice?
a) That true love comes from within and is worth fighting for
b) That love can only be found through magical means
c) That love is easy and carefree
d) That she needed to change herself to find love

Discussion

1. How important do you think self-love is when it comes to relationships?

2. In your opinion, do you believe long-distance relationships can be successful? What factors do you think contribute to the success or failure of such relationships? Share any personal experiences you may have.

3. The apothecary gave Hannah valuable advice about love. Have you ever received life-changing advice from an unexpected source? How did it impact your life or relationships?

ANSWERS

1. b) A love potion
2. b) To focus on loving herself
3. c) While Hannah was playing the piano in the park
4. b) Sean had to move to a distant city for work
5. a) That true love comes from within and is worth fighting for

Sunny with a Chance of Love

Sunny Adams, a charming **weather forecaster** with golden hair and an **infectious** smile, stood in front of the green screen at the local news station. Her name was not only a perfect fit for her profession, but also for her bright and cheerful personality. She was admired by everyone in the small town of Maplewood for her accurate predictions and her warm, friendly manner.

As Sunny finished her weather forecast for the day, she gave her **signature** wink to the camera.

"And that's the weather for today, Maplewood. I'm Sunny Adams, reminding you to always stay positive and look forward to brighter days!"

When the camera stopped rolling, she sighed and looked at her watch. Her workday had ended, but her personal life was still a mess. Her thoughts were interrupted by her friend and coworker, Janice.

"Sunny, you did an amazing job today, as always! But, girl, you need to get yourself out there and find love!" Janice said with a mischievous grin.

Sunny laughed. "Janice, I appreciate your concern, but I'm too busy with work. Besides, I'm happy being single."

Janice shook her head. "Well, if you change your mind, I know a guy who might be perfect for you. He's a friend of my cousin's, and I hear he's quite the **catch**!"

Sunny smiled politely, but she knew Janice was a **relentless matchmaker**. As she packed her belongings, she secretly wished she could find someone special on her own terms.

The next day, Sunny was at the local coffee shop, lost in her thoughts about the upcoming weather forecast. As she drank her cappuccino, she accidentally bumped into a tall, dark, and handsome man in line.

"Oh! I'm so sorry!" Sunny **stammered**, her cheeks turning pink.

The man looked down at her, his deep blue eyes sparkling. "No harm done, miss. I'm Jack, by the way." He extended his hand to Sunny.

Sunny shook his hand, feeling an **inexplicable** connection. "I'm Sunny. Nice to meet you, Jack."

As they exchanged small talk, Sunny felt her heart race. She couldn't deny the chemistry between them, but she hesitated to give in to her feelings. She was a professional woman, after all, and didn't want to be swept away by some stranger.

However, as they continued to talk, Sunny found herself drawn to Jack's intelligence and wit. He was a successful architect who had just moved to Maplewood, and he was genuinely interested in her work as a weather forecaster.

Over the next few weeks, Sunny and Jack bumped into each other more often. They shared coffee dates, long walks in the park, and laughter-filled conversations. Each meeting felt like a breath of fresh air, and Sunny couldn't ignore her growing feelings for Jack any longer.

One day, as they were walking along the riverbank, Jack stopped and looked deep into Sunny's eyes. "Sunny, I know this might sound crazy, but I think I'm falling in love with you."

Sunny's heart **fluttered**. "Jack, I've been

feeling the same way. I never thought I'd find someone who understands and appreciates me like you do."

Jack leaned in and gently kissed Sunny. The sun shone brightly on them, as if the universe itself was blessing their newfound love.

Just as Sunny and Jack's relationship was **blossoming**, a massive storm threatened Maplewood. The town turned to Sunny for guidance, and she was determined not to let them down. Working long hours at the news station, she analyzed data and prepared emergency plans to keep the community safe.

During this time, Sunny and Jack's dates became less frequent, but they still found comfort in each other's company. Jack was understanding and supportive, always there to bring her coffee or a **reassuring** hug when she needed it the most.

One evening, as the storm approached, Jack visited Sunny at the news station. She was exhausted and worried, but he managed to bring a smile to her face.

"Sunny, you're doing an amazing job. The whole town is counting on you, and I know you won't let them down."

Sunny looked at Jack, her eyes **brimming** with tears. "Thank you, Jack. Your support means the world to me."

Jack took her hand and said, "When this storm passes, let's take a trip together, just the two of us. I want to show you how much you mean to me."

Sunny's heart swelled with happiness. "I'd love that, Jack."

The storm hit Maplewood with full force, but thanks to Sunny's accurate predictions and the community's preparedness, the damage was minimal. The town breathed a collective sigh of relief as the storm clouds began to part, revealing a beautiful rainbow.

Jack took Sunny by the hand and led her outside to witness the breathtaking sight. As they stood under the rainbow, Jack whispered in her ear, "Sunny, you are the sunshine in my life, and you've brought so much love and happiness into my world. Will you be my partner in life, through storms and sunny days alike?"

Sunny looked up at Jack, her eyes glistening with tears of joy. "Yes, Jack, I will."

As they embraced, the sun shone brightly upon them, casting a warm glow on the couple who had **weathered the storm** together. The town of Maplewood would forever remember Sunny and Jack as the **epitome** of love and resilience, proving that even in the darkest of times, there's always a chance of love.

New words

- **weather forecaster** (*noun*) - A person who predicts and reports weather conditions.
- **infectious** (*adj.*) - Capable of spreading easily from person to person (usually used for describing diseases, but can also describe smiles or laughter that quickly affect others).
- **catch** (*noun*) - A person who is considered to be an attractive or desirable partner.
- **signature** (*adj.*) - Distinctive or unique; a characteristic that identifies someone or something.
- **relentless** (*adj.*) - Unyielding or persistent, continuing without stopping.
- **matchmaker** (*noun*) - A person who tries to arrange relationships between other people.
- **stammer** (verb) - To speak with sudden involuntary pauses or repetitions of sounds or words, often due to nervousness or embarrassment.

- **inexplicable** (*adj.*) - Difficult or impossible to explain or understand.
- **riverbank** (*noun*) - The land alongside a river.
- **flutter** (*verb*) - To move or beat quickly and lightly, often used to describe a feeling of excitement or nervousness.
- **blossoming** (*adj.*) - Developing or growing successfully, often used to describe relationships or feelings.
- **brimming** (*verb*) - Filled to the point of overflowing; full of a particular quality or emotion.
- **reassuring** (*adj.*) - Giving comfort or confidence; restoring a sense of security or calm.
- **weather the storm** (*idiom*) - To endure or survive a difficult or challenging situation,
- **epitome** (*noun*) - A perfect example or representation of a particular quality or type; the embodiment of something.

Test yourself

1. What is Sunny's profession?
a) Architect
b) Weather forecaster
c) Matchmaker
d) News reporter

2. How did Sunny and Jack first meet?
a) At the news station
b) In a park
c) At a local coffee shop
d) At a friend's party

3. What does Janice do to help Sunny find love?
a) Introduces her to a friend of her cousin
b) Sets her up on a blind date
c) Encourages her to join a dating website
d) Plans a surprise party

4. How does Jack support Sunny during the massive storm?
a) By helping her make emergency plans
b) By bringing her coffee and offering hugs
c) By taking her on a vacation
d) By working with her at the news station

5. What happens after the storm clears in Maplewood?
a) Sunny and Jack break up
b) Sunny and Jack get engaged
c) Sunny decides to leave the town
d) Jack proposes a vacation to celebrate

Discussion

1. What are some qualities that make Sunny and Jack a good match for each other? Can you think of any examples from you and your partner, or your friends' partners?
2. How do Sunny and Jack support each other throughout the story? How important is a partner's support to you?
3. In the story, Maplewood faces a massive storm. How does the community come together during this difficult time? Have you experienced a similar situation?
4. How do you think Sunny and Jack's relationship will continue to grow after the storm? What might their future together look like?

Answers

1. b) Weather forecaster
2. c) At a local coffee shop
3. a) Introduces her to a friend of her cousin
4. b) By bringing her coffee and offering hugs
5. b) Sunny and Jack get engaged

Journey of the Intertwined Souls

Valerie had always loved traveling. She loved to see new places, meet new people, and experience different cultures. So when she had the chance to spend a year abroad after college, she jumped at the opportunity. She visited countless cities, each one leaving a unique impression on her.

One day, while exploring a bustling street in Tokyo, Valerie **stopped in her tracks**. Across the street, she saw a man who seemed familiar. She couldn't quite place him, but there was something about him that made her heart skip a beat. She watched as he disappeared into the crowd, wondering if she would ever see him again.

JOURNEY OF THE INTERTWINED SOULS

Months passed, and Valerie continued her travels. She went to Europe, South America, and even Antarctica. In each place, she found something new to love. But no matter where she went, she couldn't let go of the memory of the man in Tokyo.

It wasn't until Valerie found herself in a small village in Tuscany that she learned the truth. There, she met an old **fortune teller** who sensed Valerie's **yearning** heart. The fortune teller told Valerie that the man she was looking for was, in fact, her soulmate, but their union would require a great **sacrifice**. Valerie felt both excited and nervous, unsure of what the future would bring.

As fate would have it, Valerie and Alex crossed paths again in Barcelona.

"Hey, I remember you from Tokyo!" the man said with a smile.

"Wow, what a coincidence! It's nice to see you again," Valerie replied, feeling a surge of excitement.

They struck up a conversation, and Valerie learned that his name was Alex. They spent the afternoon wandering around the city, laughing and chatting like old friends.

When Valerie shared the fortune teller's **prophecy** with Alex, they both agreed that they were willing to make any sacrifice for their love.

After their reunion in Barcelona, Valerie and Alex were inseparable. It was during a quiet evening in their rented apartment, when they were browsing through an old bookstore, that they stumbled upon a dusty, **leather-bound** book. The book was filled with ancient legends, stories of love, and the mysteries of the universe.

As they flipped through the pages, they discovered a tale about **soulmates** who were destined to be together, but who had to overcome a great challenge to unite their souls. The story spoke of a hidden artifact that could solidify their bond and ensure that they would never be separated.

Intrigued by the story and its parallels with the fortune teller's prophecy, Valerie and Alex decided to research further. They visited libraries and consulted experts in folklore and mythology, gradually uncovering clues about the artifact's existence and location. With each new discovery, they grew more convinced that this was the key to their future together.

One day, while **poring** over ancient **manuscripts** in the National Library of Spain, they found a map that seemed to point to the locations of various **mystical relics**. One symbol, in particular, caught their eye – a heart intertwined with an **infinity** sign. They knew that this was the artifact they were searching for, and that their quest was about to begin.

As they embarked on their journey to find the hidden artifact, Valerie and Alex were filled with a sense of purpose and excitement. They knew that the path would be filled with challenges, but they were willing to face them together, confident in their love and their destiny.

It was during their search for the artifact that Valerie and Alex truly tested the strength of their bond. They faced physical and emotional **obstacles**, and their commitment to one another was challenged at every turn. However, these trials only served to bring them closer together, deepening their love and proving that they were truly meant to be.

At last, they found the artifact hidden in a cave deep in the Amazon rainforest. As they held it in their hands, they felt a powerful surge of energy, and a mystical bond formed between their souls. They knew that their love was now eternal, and they would never be apart again.

However, the sacrifice the fortune teller mentioned became clear – they had to give up their ability to travel the world. Valerie and Alex were faced with a difficult choice, but they knew that their love was worth more than any journey they could take.

Hand in hand, they returned to Valerie's small hometown in the Midwest. There, they settled down and built a life together, filling their home with treasures and memories from their travels. They opened a small café, where they shared their love for different cultures and cuisines with the townspeople.

Years passed, and Valerie and Alex's love only grew stronger. They were a living testament to the power of love and the sacrifices one must make for it. While they could no longer travel the world, their love had created a new world around them – one filled with adventure, passion, and the magic of unexpected encounters.

In the end, Valerie realized that the most important journey of her life had not been to the far corners of the earth but rather the journey to find her soulmate and the love they shared. With Alex by her side, she had found her true home, and they had created their own world of adventure right where they were.

New words

- **fortune teller** (*noun*) - a person who claims to predict the future
- **yearning** (*noun*) - a strong feeling of wanting or needing something
- **prophecy** (*noun*) - a prediction about what will happen in the future
- **soulmate** (*noun*) - a person who is perfectly suited to be with another person in a romantic relationship
- **sacrifice** (*noun*) - the act of giving up something important or valuable for the sake of something else
- **artifact** (*noun*) - an object made by a human being, typically from an earlier time
- **mystical** (*adj.*) - having a spiritual or mysterious quality
- **leather-bound** (*adj.*) - having a cover made of leather

- **mythology** (*noun*) - a collection of myths, especially one belonging to a particular culture
- **manuscript** (*noun*) - a handwritten or typed document, especially a book or other written work before it is printed
- **relic** (*noun*) - an object or item that has survived from an earlier time and is often valued for its historical significance
- **infinity** (*noun*) - the state or quality of being endless or limitless
- **poring** (*verb*) - to read or study something carefully and attentively
- **obstacle** (*noun*): something that makes it difficult to achieve a goal or complete a task

Test yourself

1. What was Valerie's favorite activity?
a) Painting
b) Traveling
c) Cooking
d) Reading

2. Where did Valerie first see the man who seemed familiar to her?
a) Tokyo
b) Paris
c) Sydney
d) Marrakech

3. What did the old fortune teller in Tuscany tell Valerie about the man she was looking for?
a) He was her brother.
b) He was her soulmate.
c) He was her enemy.

4. What was the great sacrifice Valerie and Alex had to make for their love?
a) They had to give up their families.
b) They had to give up their ability to travel the world.
c) They had to give up their careers.

5. Where did Valerie and Alex find the hidden artifact that would unite their souls?
a) In a cave in the Amazon rainforest
b) In the mountains of Peru
c) In the deserts of Egypt
d) In a temple in Borneo

Discussion

1. Do you believe in the concept of soulmates? Why or why not? Can there be more than one soulmate for a person, or is it limited to just one perfect match?
2. In the story, Valerie and Alex had to make a significant sacrifice to be together. What are some sacrifices you think people might have to make in real-life relationships? Are there any sacrifices that you think are too great to make for love?
3. How do you think traveling and experiencing different cultures can impact a person's worldview and personal growth? Do you have any personal experiences where traveling has changed your perspective on life or relationships?

Answers

1. b) Traveling
2. a) Tokyo
3. b) He was her soulmate
4. b) The had to give up their ability to travel the world.
5. a) In a cave in the Amazon rainforest

Great work! Why not check out our other books? Here are a few you might like:

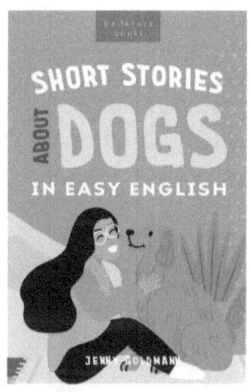

Available now in all major online bookstores.

FREE BONUS STORY

Finished these stories and still want more?

Visit:
www.bellanovabooks.com/romance-bonus

to receive your **free bonus story.** Happy reading!

Thanks for reading this book. We hope you've had a great time with it and improved your English!

As authors, we're always eager to hear what you think, so we'd love it if you could take a moment to **leave a review**. Your honest feedback helps us improve our writing and also helps other readers decide if this book is right for them. Plus, we'd just really appreciate it!

SCAN ME

Join us!

Are you ready to take your English learning journey to the next level? Then join our private Facebook community of fellow learners! It's a friendly and supportive space where you can share, learn, and practice English.

Just scan the QR code and you'll be taken straight to our Facebook page. See you there!

facebook.com/groups/learnenglishhub

www.ingramcontent.com/pod-product-compliance
Lightning Source LLC
LaVergne TN
LVHW040149080526
838202LV00042B/3086